JESUS

A four-week course to help adults learn about and grow closer to Jesus.

by
Paul Woods

Apply·It·To·Life™
Adult

BIBLE CURRICULUM
from *Group*

Group
Loveland, Colorado

Apply·It·To·Life™ Adult BIBLE CURRICULUM

Group®

Jesus
Copyright © 1995 Group Publishing, Inc.

All rights reserved. No part of this book may be reproduced in any manner whatsoever without prior written permission from the publisher, except where noted on handouts and in the case of brief quotations embodied in critical articles and reviews. For information, write Permissions, Group Publishing, Inc., Dept. BK, Box 481, Loveland, CO 80539.

Credits
Editor: Stephen Parolini
Creative Products Director: Joani Schultz
Cover Designer: Liz Howe
Interior Designer: Kathy Benson
Illustrator: Sam Thiewes
Cover Illustrator: DeWain Stoll

ISBN 1-55945-500-4

10 9 8 7 6 5 4 3 2 1   04 03 02 01 00 99 98 97 96 95

Printed in the United States of America.

CONTENTS

INTRODUCTION	5
What Is Apply-It-To-Life™ Adult Bible Curriculum?	5
What Makes Apply-It-To-Life Adult Bible Curriculum Unique?	5
How to Use Apply-It-To-Life Adult Bible Curriculum	10
Course Introduction: Jesus	13
Publicity Page	15

LESSON 1 17

God With Us
Jesus is God, but for our benefit he also became fully human.

LESSON 2 29

A Religious Rebel
Jesus challenged wrongdoing and stood up for what was right.

LESSON 3 41

Our Triumphant Lord
We have hope because Jesus conquered death.

LESSON 4 51

Teacher for All Time
Jesus' teachings can have a powerful impact on our lives.

FELLOWSHIP AND OUTREACH SPECIALS 63

Introduction

WHAT IS APPLY-IT-TO-LIFE™ ADULT BIBLE CURRICULUM?

Apply-It-To-Life™ Adult Bible Curriculum is a series of four-week study courses designed to help you facilitate powerful lessons that will help class members grow in faith. Use this course with
- Sunday school classes,
- home study groups,
- weekday Bible study groups,
- men's Bible studies,
- women's Bible studies, and
- family classes.

The variety of courses gives the adult student a broad coverage of topical, life-related issues and significant biblical topics. In addition, as the name of the series implies, every lesson helps the adult student apply Scripture to his or her life.

Each course in Apply-It-To-Life Adult Bible Curriculum provides four lessons on different aspects of one topic. In each course, you also receive Fellowship and Outreach Specials connected to the month's topic. They provide suggestions for building closer relationships in your class, outreach activities, and even a party idea!

WHAT MAKES APPLY-IT-TO-LIFE ADULT BIBLE CURRICULUM UNIQUE?

Teaching as Jesus Taught

Jesus was a master teacher. With Apply-It-To-Life Adult Bible Curriculum, you'll use the same teaching methods and principles that Jesus used:

- **Active Learning.** Think back on an important lesson you've learned in life. Did you learn it from reading about it? from hearing about it? from something you did? Chances are, the most important lessons you've learned came from something you experienced. That's what active learning is—learning by doing. Active learning leads students through activities and experiences that help them understand important principles, messages, and ideas. It's a discovery process that helps people internalize and remember what they learn.

Jesus often used active learning. One of the most vivid examples is his washing of his disciples' feet. In Apply-It-To-Life Adult Bible Curriculum, the teacher might remove his or her shoes and socks then read aloud the foot-washing passage from John 13, or the teacher might choose to actually wash people's feet. Participants won't soon forget it. Active learning uses simple activities to teach profound lessons.

● **Interactive Learning.** Interactive learning means learning through small-group interaction and discussion. While it may seem to be a simple concept, it's radically new to many churches that have stuck with a lecture format or large-group discussion for so long. With interactive learning, each person is actively involved in discovering God's truth through talking with other people about God's Word. Interactive learning is discussion with a difference. It puts people in pairs, trios, or foursomes to involve everyone in the learning experience. It takes active learning a step further by having people who have gone through an experience teach others what they've learned.

Jesus often helped cement the learning from an experience by questioning people—sometimes in small groups—about what had happened. He regularly questioned his followers and his opponents, forcing them to think and to discuss among themselves what he was teaching them. After washing his disciples' feet, the first thing Jesus did was ask the disciples if they understood what he had done. After the "foot washing" activity, the teacher might form small groups and have people discuss how they felt when the leader removed his or her shoes and socks. Then group members could compare those feelings and the learning involved to what the disciples must have experienced.

● **Biblical Depth.** Apply-It-To-Life Adult Bible Curriculum recognizes that most adults are ready to go below the surface to better understand the deeper truths of the Bible. Therefore, the activities and studies go beyond an "easy answer" approach to Christian education and lead adults to grapple with difficult issues from a biblical perspective.

Each lesson begins by giving the teacher resource material on the Bible passages covered in the study. In the Bible Basis, you'll find information that will help you understand the Scriptures you're dealing with. Within the class-time section of the lesson, thought-provoking activities and discussions lead adults to new depths of biblical understanding. Bible Insights within the lesson give pertinent information that will bring the

Bible to life for you and your class members. In-class handouts give adults significant Bible information and challenge them to search for and discover biblical truths for themselves. Finally, the "For Even Deeper Discussion" sections provide questions that will lead your class members to new and deeper levels of insight and application.

No one questions the depth of Jesus' teachings or the effectiveness of his teaching methods. This curriculum follows Jesus' example and helps people probe the depths of the Bible in a way no other adult curriculum does.

● **Bible Application.** Jesus didn't stop with helping people understand truth. For him, teaching took the learner beyond understanding to application. It wasn't enough that the rich young ruler knew all the right answers. Jesus wanted him to take action on what he knew. In the same way, Apply-It-To-Life Adult Bible Curriculum encourages a response in people's lives. That's why this curriculum is called "Apply-It-To-Life"! Depth of understanding means little if the truths of Scripture don't zing into people's hearts. Each lesson brings home one point and encourages people to consider the changes they might make in response.

● **One Purpose.** In each study, every activity works toward communicating and applying the same point. People may discover other new truths, but the study doesn't load them down with a mass of information. Sometimes less is more. When lessons try to teach too much, they often fail to teach anything. Even Jesus limited his teaching to what he felt people could really learn and apply (John 16:12). Apply-It-To-Life Adult Bible Curriculum makes sure that class members thoroughly understand and apply one point each week.

● **Variety.** People appreciate variety. Jesus constantly varied his teaching methods. One day he would have a serious discussion with his disciples about who he was and another day he'd baffle them by turning water into wine. What he didn't do was allow them to become bored with what he had to teach them.

Any kind of study can become less than exciting if the leader and students do everything the same way week after week. Apply-It-To-Life Adult Bible Curriculum varies activities and approaches to keep everyone's interest level high each week. In one class, you might have people in small groups "put themselves in the disciples' sandals" and experience something of the confusion of Jesus' death and resurrection. In another lesson, class members may experience problems in communication and examine how such problems can damage relationships.

To meet adults' varied needs, the courses cover a wide range of topics such as Jesus, knowing God's will, communication, taking faith to work, and highlights of Bible books. One month you may choose to study a family or personal faith issue; the next month you may cover a biblical topic such as the book of John.

● **Relevance.** People today want to know how to live successfully right now. They struggle with living as authentic Christians at work, in the family, and in the community. Most churchgoing adults want to learn about the Bible, but not merely for the sake of having greater Bible knowledge. They want to know how the Bible can help them live faithful lives—how it can help them face the difficulties of living in today's culture. Apply-It-To-Life Adult Bible Curriculum bridges the gap between biblical truth and the "real world" issues of people's lives. Jesus didn't discuss with his followers the eschatological significance of Ezekiel's wheels, and Apply-It-To-Life Bible Curriculum won't either! Courses and studies in this curriculum focus on the real needs of people and help them discover answers in Scripture that will help meet those needs.

● **A Nonthreatening Atmosphere.** In many adult classes, people feel intimidated because they're new Christians or because they don't have the Bible knowledge they think they should have. Jesus sometimes intimidated those who opposed him, but he consistently treated his followers with understanding and respect. We want people in church to experience the same understanding and respect Jesus' followers experienced. With Apply-It-To-Life Adult Bible Curriculum, no one is embarrassed for not knowing or understanding as much as someone else. In fact, the interactive learning process minimizes the differences between those with vast Bible knowledge and those with little Bible knowledge. Lessons often begin with nonthreatening, sharing questions and move slowly toward more depth. Whatever their level of knowledge or commitment, class members will work together to discover biblical truths that can affect their lives.

● **A Group That Cares.** Jesus began his ministry by choosing a group of 12 people who learned from him together. That group practically lived together—sharing one another's hurts, joys, and ambitions. Sometimes Jesus divided the 12 into smaller groups and worked with just three or four at a time.

Studies have shown that many adults today long for a close-knit group of people with whom they can share personal needs and joys. And people interact more freely when they feel accepted in a group. Activities in this curriculum will help class members get to know one another better and care for one another more as they study the Bible and apply its truths to their lives. As people reveal their thoughts and feelings to one another, they'll grow closer and develop more commitment to the group and to each other. And they'll be encouraging one another along the way!

● **An Element of Delight.** We don't often think about Jesus' ministry in this way, but there certainly were times he brought fun and delight to his followers. Remember the time he raised Peter's mother-in-law? or the time he sat happily with children on his lap? How about the joy and excitement at his triumphal entry into Jerusalem? or the time he helped fishing disciples catch a boatload of fish—after they'd fished all night with no success?

People learn more when they're having fun. So within Apply-It-To-Life Adult Bible Curriculum, elements of fun and delight pop up often. And sometimes adding fun is as simple as using a carrot for a pretend microphone!

Taking the Fear Out of Teaching

Teachers love Apply-It-To-Life Adult Bible Curriculum because it makes teaching much less stressful. Lessons in this curriculum

● **are easy to teach.** Interactive learning frees the teacher from being a dispenser of information to serve as a facilitator of learning. Teachers can spend class time guiding people to discover and apply biblical truths. The studies provide clear, understandable Bible background; easy-to-prepare learning experiences; and powerful, thought-provoking discussion questions.

● **can be prepared quickly.** Lessons in Apply-It-To-Life Adult Bible Curriculum are logical and clear. There's no sorting through tons of information to figure out the lesson. In 30 minutes, a busy teacher can easily read a lesson and prepare to teach it. In addition, optional and For Extra Time activities allow the teacher to tailor the lesson to the class. And the thorough instructions and questions will guide even an inexperienced teacher through each powerful lesson.

● **let everyone share in the class's success.** With Apply-It-To-Life Bible Curriculum, the teacher is one of the participants. The teacher still guides the class, but the burden is not as heavy. Everyone participates and adds to the study's effectiveness. So when the study has an impact, everyone shares in that success.

● **lead the teacher to new discoveries.** Each lesson is designed to help the teacher first discover a biblical truth. And most teachers will make additional discoveries as they prepare each lesson. In class, the teacher will discover even more as other adults share what they have found. As with any type of teaching, the teacher will likely learn more than anyone else in the class!

● **provide relevant information to class members.**

Photocopiable handouts are designed to help people better understand or interpret Bible passages. And the handouts make teaching easier because the teacher can often refer to them for small-group discussion questions and instructions.

HOW TO USE APPLY-IT-TO-LIFE ADULT BIBLE CURRICULUM

First familiarize yourself with an Apply-It-To-Life Adult Bible Curriculum lesson. The following explanations will help you understand how the lesson elements work together.

Lesson Elements

- The **Opening** maps out the lesson's agenda and introduces your class to the topic for the session. Sometimes this activity will help people get better acquainted as they begin to explore the topic together.

- The **Bible Exploration and Application** activities will help people discover what the Bible says about the topic and how the lesson's point applies to their lives. In these varied activities, class members find answers to the "So what?" question. Through active and interactive learning methods, people will discover the relevance of the Scriptures and commit to growing closer to God.

  You may use either one or both of the options in this section. They are designed to stand alone or to work together. Both present the same point in different ways. "For Even Deeper Discussion" questions appear at the end of each activity in this section. Use these questions whenever you feel they might be particularly helpful for your class.

- The **Closing** pulls everything in the lesson together and often funnels the lesson's message into a time of reflection and prayer.

- The **For Extra Time** section is just that. Use it when you've completed the lesson and still have time left or when you've used one Bible Exploration and Application option and don't have time to do the other. Or you might plan to use it instead of another option.

When you put all the sections together, you get a lesson that's fun and easy to teach. Plus, participants will learn truths they'll remember and apply to their daily lives.

About the Questions and Answers

The answers given after discussion questions are responses participants *might* give. They aren't the only answers or the "right" answers. However, you can use them to spark discussion.

Real life doesn't always allow us to give the "right" answers. That's why some of the responses given are negative or controversial. If someone responds negatively, don't be shocked. Accept the person and use the opportunity to explore other perspectives on the issue.

To get more out of your discussions, use follow-up inquiries such as
- Tell me more.
- What do you mean by that?
- What makes you feel that way?

Guidelines for a Successful Adult Class

- **Be a facilitator, not a lecturer.** Apply-It-To-Life Adult Bible Curriculum is student-based rather than teacher-based. Your job is to direct the activities and facilitate the discussions. You become a choreographer of sorts: someone who gets everyone else involved in the discussion and keeps the discussion on track.

- **Teach adults how to form small groups.** Help adults discover the benefits of small-group discussions by assisting them in forming groups of four, three, or two—whatever the activity calls for. Small-group sharing allows for more discussion and involvement by all participants. It's not as threatening or scary to open up to two people as it would be to 20 or 200!

Some leaders decide not to form small groups because they want to hear everybody's ideas. The intention is good, but some people just won't talk in a large group. Use a "report back" time after small-group discussions to gather the best responses from all groups.

When you form small groups, don't always let people choose those right around them. Try creative group-forming methods to help everyone in the class get to know one another. For example, tell class members: find three other people wearing the same color you are; join two other people who like the same music you do; locate three others who shop at the same grocery store you do; find one who was born the same month as you; choose three who like the same season as you, and so on. If you have fun with it, your class will, too!

● **Encourage relationship building.** George Barna, in his insightful book about the church, *The Frog in the Kettle,* explains that adults today have a strong need to develop friendships. In a society of high-tech toys, "personal" computers, and lonely commutes, people long for positive human contact. That's where our church classes and groups can jump in. Help adults form friendships through your class. What's discovered in a classroom setting will be better applied when friends support each other outside the classroom. In fact, the relationships begun in your class may be as important as the truths you help your adults learn.

● **Be flexible.** Sometimes your class will complete every activity in the lesson with great success and wonderful learning. But what should you do if people go off on a tangent? or they get stuck in one of the activities? What if you don't have time to finish the lesson?

Don't panic. People learn best when they are interested and engaged in meaningful discussion, when they move at their own pace. And if you get through even one activity, your class will discover the point for the whole lesson. So relax. It's OK if you don't get everything done. Try to get to the Closing in every lesson, since its purpose is to bring closure to the topic for the week. But if you don't, don't sweat it!

● **Expect the unexpected.** Active learning is an adventure that doesn't always take you where you think you're going. Don't be surprised if things don't go exactly the way you'd planned. Be open to the different directions the Holy Spirit may lead your class. When something goes wrong or an unexpected emotion is aroused, take advantage of the teachable moment. Ask probing questions; follow up on someone's deep need or concern. Those moments are often the best opportunities for learning that come our way.

● **Participate—and encourage participation.** Apply-It-To-Life Adult Bible Curriculum is only as interactive as you and your class make it. Learning arises out of dialogue. People need to grapple with and verbalize their questions and discoveries. Jump into discussions yourself, but don't "take over." Encourage everyone to participate. You can facilitate smooth discussions by using "active listening" responses such as rephrasing and summing up what's been said. If people seem stumped, use the possible responses after each question to spark further discussion. You may feel like a cheerleader at times, but your efforts will be worth it. The more people participate, the more they'll discover God's truths for themselves.

● **Trust the Holy Spirit.** All the previous six guidelines and the instructions in the lessons will be irrelevant if you ignore the presence of God in your classroom. God sent the Holy Spirit as our helper. As you use this curriculum, ask the Holy Spirit to help you facilitate the lessons. And ask the Holy Spirit to direct your class toward God's truth. Trust that God's Spirit can work through each person's discoveries, not just the teacher's.

How to Use This Course

Before the Four-Week Session
- Read the Course Introduction and This Course at a Glance (pp. 13-14).
- Decide how you'll use the art on the Publicity Page (p. 15) to publicize the course. Prepare fliers, newsletter articles, and posters as needed.
- Look at the Fellowship and Outreach Specials (p. 63) and decide which ones you'll use.

Before Each Lesson
- Read the one-sentence Point, the Objectives, and the Bible Basis for the lesson. The Bible Basis provides background information on the lesson's passages and shows how those passages relate to people today.
- Choose which activities you'll use from the lesson. Remember, it's not important to do every activity. Pick the ones that best fit your group and time allotment.
- Gather necessary supplies. They're listed in This Lesson at a Glance.
- Read each section of the lesson. Adjust activities as necessary to fit your class size and meeting room, but be careful not to delete all the activity. People learn best when they're actively involved in the learning process.

COURSE INTRODUCTION: JESUS

When you think about Jesus, what do you think of? a baby in a manger? a teacher on a hillside? a dying man on a cross? a victorious resurrected Lord? Who is this man who can calm the sea, heal the sick, cast out demons, love his enemies, and forgive sins?

Most Christians think about Jesus occasionally. But our picture of Jesus is usually incomplete. We know bits and pieces about his life. And we know that our goal is to be like Christ. But there is always more to know—more to understand.

Also, the people around us have many other pictures of Jesus. Some say he was just a great man—that he taught good things, but wasn't really God. Or they say that stories about Jesus are just chapters of a larger myth—a myth that allows people to do the impossible—rise from the dead.

But if we believe the Bible is trustworthy, we have a reliable record of who Jesus was and is. And that record can be a tremendous encouragement as we face the struggles of our daily lives. As we learn more about who Jesus is, we'll grow closer to him. And we'll gain confidence and hope in our future as we trust the one who lived, died, and rose from the dead because of his love for us.

This four-week series will help adults better understand who Jesus is. Participants will explore how knowing Jesus and what he's done for us can change our lives. And they'll be challenged to live their lives in gratitude for what God, in his incredible love, has done for us through Christ.

This Course at a Glance

Before you dive into the lessons, familiarize yourself with each lesson's point. Then read the Scripture passages.

- Study them as a background to the lessons.
- Use them as a basis for your personal devotions.
- Think about how they relate to adults' circumstances today.

Lesson 1: God With Us
The Point: Jesus is God, but for our benefit he also became fully human.
Bible Basis: Galatians 4:3-5 and John 1:1-18

Lesson 2: A Religious Rebel
The Point: Jesus rebelled at wrongdoing and stood up for what was right.
Bible Basis: Matthew 23:1-32 and John 2:12-22

Lesson 3: Our Triumphant Lord
The Point: We have hope because Jesus conquered death.
Bible Basis: John 20:1-8; Romans 6:1-14; and Romans 8:31-39

Lesson 4: Teacher for All Time
The Point: Jesus' teachings can have a powerful impact on our lives.
Bible Basis: James 1:22-25

PUBLICITY PAGE

Grab your congregation's attention! Add the vital details to the ready-made flier below, photocopy it, and use it to advertise this course on Jesus. Insert the flier in your bulletins. Enlarge it to make posters. Splash the art or anything else from this page in newsletters, bulletins, or even on postcards! It's that simple.

The art from this page is also available on Group's MinistryNet™ computer on-line resource for you to manipulate on your computer. Call 800-447-1070 for information.

A four-week adult course on knowing Jesus better.

COME TO

ON

AT

Jesus

COME LEARN MORE ABOUT THE ONE WHO LIVED, DIED, AND ROSE FROM THE DEAD— FOR YOU!

Apply·It·To·Life™
Adult
BIBLE CURRICULUM
from Group

Permission to photocopy this page granted for local church use. Copyright © Group Publishing, Inc., Box 481, Loveland, CO 80539.

Lesson 1
God With Us

◄ **THE POINT**

Jesus is God, but for our benefit he also became fully human.

OBJECTIVES

Participants will
- examine differing perceptions of Jesus,
- explore why Jesus came as a human, and
- consider how God's sending of Jesus should affect our lives.

BIBLE BASIS

Look up the following Scriptures. Then read the following background sections to see how the passages relate to adults today.

In **John 1:1-18,** the author describes God becoming human.

JOHN 1:1-18

As John describes the "Word" that was with God from the beginning of time, he is describing Jesus.

The Greek noun, *logos,* which is translated "Word" in John 1:1, 14, has much deeper connotations than our understanding of "word." *Logos* comes from the verb *lego,* which means "to collect" or "pick out." *Logos,* then, suggests to us "picked out" or "collected" thoughts—a complete concept, expressing the mind of the author. So when John speaks of Jesus as the Word, we can take that to mean Jesus is the complete concept of who God is. He's the ultimate revelation of God himself to human beings. In Jesus, God has shown us his collected thoughts, which he picked out as the specific things we need to know to build a relationship with him.

And not only does this "Word" reveal God to us, but this verse also tells us that he *is* God. The Greek structure in John 1:1 lets us know that though Jesus isn't all there is of God, he himself is all God.

Since Jesus is God, he has always existed. He was instrumental in creation; he is the giver of life. Yet he came to bring light to a dark world—becoming one of its inhabitants. John tells us that God became a human in Jesus. This act we call the Incarnation—a word that comes from the Latin for "becoming human." John also emphasizes that Jesus came to make a difference in our lives. He came to let us know more fully who God is. He came so that you and your students might live eternally—and abundantly!

It's difficult—if not impossible with our finite minds—to understand Jesus' relationship with the Father. How could Jesus be fully God and fully human at the same time? We may not understand it, but we can accept this truth in faith, trusting the God who has done so much for us.

GALATIANS 4:3-5

In **Galatians 4:3-5,** Paul is explaining how God made it possible for us to be his children. During Paul's first visit, when he founded the church in Galatia, he taught them that repentance and belief in Jesus were the only keys to receiving forgiveness and eternal life. But after that time, other teachers had come to Galatia insisting that to be a Christian, you first had to observe all the Jewish laws. They taught that to be a true child of God, you had to follow lots of rules and regulations.

Paul wanted the Galatians—and us—to know that we can became children of God only through what God did for us in Jesus. And he explained why Jesus alone was able to do that for us. These verses state that Jesus was divine—he had existed in heaven with the Father before the Incarnation. And he was also human—"born of a woman."

Had Jesus been anything less than fully God and fully human, he couldn't have done what he did. If he had not been human, he couldn't have experienced the same temptations and feelings we all have—his sinlessness would've meant little. He couldn't relate to us as our advocate. He couldn't have taken the sins of humanity on himself. If Jesus had not been God, he couldn't have lived a sinless life, qualifying him to be an innocent sacrifice for us. And he couldn't have defeated sin and death once and for all, as he did when he died on the cross and rose from the dead.

Without God's incredible gift of his Son, we'd have no hope of a relationship with God. Because he loves us, he sent Jesus as the unique God-man. And because God has proved how much he loves them, your students can learn to trust him and obey him in every moment, every aspect of their lives.

Unfortunately, we get caught up in our activities and busyness and often don't take time to think about what God has done for us. And we begin to take it for granted that God sent Jesus to earth on our behalf.

But God did an incredibly loving thing in coming to our world as a human. When we apply that truth to our lives, we're changed forever. We seek to serve the one who loves us and we learn to obey and trust him more fully.

THIS LESSON AT A GLANCE

Section	Minutes	What Participants Will Do	Supplies
OPENING	up to 10	**JESUS AND ME**—Use familiar objects to describe themselves and Jesus.	
BIBLE EXPLORATION AND APPLICATION	20 to 30	☐ Option 1: **TO TEACH A GOLDFISH**—Create a plan to "save" a goldfish and discuss God's plan in Galatians 4:3-5.	One goldfish in a bowl, Bibles, newsprint and markers or chalkboard and chalk
	15 to 25	☐ Option 2: **DIVINITY DEBATE**—Present distorted views of Christ and discuss the biblical view of Christ as shown in Galatians 4:4-5.	Bibles, "Jesus—Human and Divine" handout (p. 26)
CLOSING	up to 5	**WHAT NOW?**—Share with a partner how they will respond to what God has done for us through Jesus.	
FOR EXTRA TIME	up to 10	**HIDDEN IDENTITIES**—Hear descriptions of objects, blindly examine them, and then look at them to determine what they are.	Bible, various objects

OPENING

Jesus and Me
(up to 10 minutes)

As you begin the class, tell adults what they'll be learning in today's lesson. Use the following statement or your own summary of the main point: **Welcome to the first week of a four-week course on getting to know Christ. Jesus is at the very center of the Christian faith, and we talk about him a lot. Yet it seems we can always discover more about the God-man who died that we might live. In this study, we're going to examine several aspects of Jesus' life and what that means for our lives today. This course will help us understand Jesus better. And we'll be challenged to serve God more diligently because of what he's done for us.**

▶ **To begin this course, we're going to explore how Jesus is God yet for our benefit he became fully human.**

Open with prayer. Then form groups of no more than eight. Have each group form a circle. Ask each adult to come up with an object from his or her pocket, purse, or billfold that best represents who he or she is. For example, someone might hold up keys and say, "I'm a chauffeur for my kids." After everyone in the circle has had a turn, go around the circle again, having each adult come up with an object to represent who Jesus is to him or her. For example, someone might hold up a tissue and say, "Jesus is my source of comfort."

When the groups are finished, have them discuss the following questions. To help groups keep track of the questions, you might want to write them on a chalkboard or newsprint.

Ask:

● **How were our descriptions of ourselves and Jesus similar?** (Jesus was a hard worker, and so am I; Jesus cared about people and I do, too.)

● **How were they different?** (Jesus is far above us; we are human and he is God.)

● **What's significant about the way our descriptions of Jesus differed from our descriptions of ourselves?** (We are limited by being human and Jesus isn't; Jesus is God; we're merely humans trying to imitate him.)

After a few minutes of group discussion, have volunteers share their groups' insights with the rest of the class.

Say: **We all had different descriptions of ourselves and of Jesus. That's OK. We're all different, and we all see Jesus a bit differently. But there are some things about Jesus that relate to core Christian beliefs, and we're going to be studying those things**

THE POINT ▶

TEACHER TIP

This activity could lead to lots of laughter. Let it! It's part of the fun of getting to know one another.

Together

20 LESSON 1

this week. ▶ Today we're going to focus on how Jesus is God, but he was also fully human. ◀ **THE POINT**

BIBLE EXPLORATION AND APPLICATION

☐ **OPTION 1:**
To Teach a Goldfish
(20 to 30 minutes)

Set the goldfish bowl in front of the class. Form groups of three or four. Say: **The task of each group is to come up with a way to teach this goldfish that he must not jump out of this bowl or he will die. We don't want to frighten the fish or restrict him from jumping out, but we want to teach him that jumping out would almost certainly result in his death. Think creatively—don't be limited by what you perceive as "possible." In your groups, appoint a reporter (to report your plan to the rest of the class) and an encourager (to encourage everyone to contribute ideas). Your groups have three minutes to come up with a plan.**

After three minutes, have groups report their ideas. Then ask:

● **Which plan do you think has the greatest chance of succeeding? Why?**

● **As you worked in your groups, what problems did you have?** (It was frustrating; there was no way to do it.)

● **How might your situation compare to God's situation as he prepared a plan to rescue us?** (He had to have a way to convince humans of the truth; he wanted to save us.)

Have someone read Galatians 4:3-5. Ask:

● **What was the plan God carried out in his situation?** (He sent Jesus to be born of a woman; he saved us through Jesus' death.)

● **How do you think God's plan would have been different had he been trying to save goldfish instead of humans?** (He would have sent Jesus as a goldfish; he would have sent a message goldfish could understand.)

● **What is the significance of God's coming to earth as a human?** (He could speak as one of us; he could die for our sins.)

Form four groups. A group can be as few as two people. In each group, have one person be the reader, another be the reporter, and all others be discoverers (to discover how the question can be answered from the passage). Assign each group one of the following passages: Matthew 4:1-11; John 11:28-44; Acts 2:22-33; and Romans 5:6-11.

BIBLE INSIGHT

If Jesus had not been sinless, he could not have died as a sacrifice for our sins. Old Testament law required that a sacrifice be perfect. For example, a lamb for sacrifice was to be "perfect"—not having any visible or known defect. The perfect sacrifice symbolized the perfect one taking on the sins of the imperfect ones and paying the penalty for them. If Jesus had sinned, he would have been sentenced to die for his own sins—just as we are—and he could not have taken our sins upon himself.

LESSON 1

The Point

TEACHER TIP

It's important that you say The Point as it's written or in your own words in each activity. Stating it repeatedly helps adults remember it and apply it to their lives.

Say: We know that Jesus is God, but he also became fully human. Why would the Creator, the all-powerful God, stoop to becoming a lowly human being? In your groups, read your passage and discuss this question:

- What could God do only by becoming a human?

As groups study their passages, write the question on a chalkboard or newsprint. After a few minutes of discussion, bring the class back together and have groups read their passages aloud and report their insights. As they report, have a volunteer write their answers under the question on the chalkboard or newsprint.

When you have a good list of insights, re-form groups and discuss the following questions. Allow just one minute for discussion on each question. Ask:

- Why would God go through what he did in becoming a human? (Because of his love; because he wanted to save us.)
- What's wrong with believing that Jesus was a great teacher but wasn't God? (It makes Jesus out to be a liar; it makes his death on the cross meaningless.)
- Why is it important to believe that Jesus was actually a human as well as God? (If he weren't human, he couldn't have died for humans; he couldn't relate to our temptations.)
- How does Jesus' having experienced what we experience as humans affect how we relate to him? (We know he's for real; he knows how tough it is to resist temptation.)

After groups have discussed all four questions, bring everyone back together and let volunteers share their groups' answers on each question.

Say: **God's love for us goes beyond our understanding. But we do know that he loves us because of what he has done for us.**

Ask the whole class:

- How should what God did for us affect our attitude toward obeying him? (We should obey him out of gratitude; we should want to please him.)
- Knowing what God did for us, how are our lives different from the lives of people who don't believe in him? (We obey him gratefully; we live for him.)

FOR Even Deeper DISCUSSION

Form groups of no more than four to discuss the following questions:

- If you believe in God, what difference does it make what you believe about Jesus?

● How would your life be different if you didn't believe that Jesus was really God and human?
● How will your life be different as a result of the reminder you've received in this lesson?

■ ■

☐ **OPTION 2:**
Divinity Debate
(15 to 25 minutes)

Form four groups. If you already have formed four groups, use the same groups. Give each person a copy of the "Jesus—Human and Divine" handout (p. 26) and assign one view from the handout to each group. Have groups follow the instructions at the top of the handout to prepare a one-minute presentation defending the view they've been assigned.

Allow groups three minutes to prepare, then have groups give their presentations.

After each presentation, ask the entire group:
● **How would you react to someone who really believed this view?**
● **What positive aspects does this view contain?**
● **What's wrong with this view?**

After all the presentations have been completed, ask:
● **How does learning about these distorted views help us maintain a biblical view of Jesus?** (It helps us watch out for false views; it helps us refine our view.)

Have your class read Galatians 4:4-5. Ask:
● **What is the biblical view of Jesus?**

As you discuss this question, encourage adults to jot down notes about key points in the True View section at the bottom of the "Jesus—Human and Divine" handout. If you have time, review each of the passages listed in that section (same as used in Option 1). Feel free to add interesting information from the Bible Basis section of this lesson.

● **Why is it important that we hold a biblical view of Jesus?** (So that we don't teach falsely; because if we don't, we may not really be Christian.)

Say: **It's important that we hold a biblical view of who Jesus was and is, because that affects our relationship with him and our outlook on the Christian life.** ▷ **We must always remember that Jesus is God, yet for our benefit he became fully human.**

If you have 24 or more people, form eight or more groups in multiples of four. Be sure no group has fewer than three or more than six participants. With fewer than three, individuals may feel uncomfortable or threatened. With more than six, it is too easy for some people to not participate at all.

Just in case you aren't familiar with the names of the groups on the handout, here are the pronunciations: Ebionites (EH-bee-uh-nights), Docetists (DAHS-a-tists), Arians (AIR-ee-ans), Nestorians (Neh-STORE-ee-ans).

◀ THE POINT

LESSON 1 23

FOR *Even Deeper* DISCUSSION

Form groups of no more than four and discuss the following questions:

● How does a person's view of Christ's humanity and divinity affect his or her outlook on the Christian life?

● What does the Incarnation tell us about God?

● What does the Incarnation tell us about God's view of us?

Have groups report highlights of their discussions to the rest of the class.

APPLY•IT•TO LIFE THIS WEEK

The "Apply-It-To-Life This Week" handout helps adults further explore the issues uncovered in today's class.

Give each adult a copy of the handout (p. 27) before they leave and encourage them to take time during the week to explore the questions and activities listed on the handout.

CLOSING

What Now?

(up to 5 minutes)

Form pairs. Have partners individually complete the following two sentences and then share why they completed the sentences the way they did.

● **If Jesus is truly God and truly man, that means that I . . .**

● **One thing I will do to get to know Jesus better is . . .**

After partners have shared, have them tell each other something they appreciate about their partner's understanding of Jesus. If partners don't know each other well, have them briefly tell about their own relationship with Christ.

Say: **Even the greatest biblical scholars learn more about Jesus every day. We may not know everything about Christ, ▶ but we do know that Jesus is God, yet he became fully human for our benefit. We've examined why God sent Jesus, and we've discussed what that should mean in our lives. Now it's up to us to do something about it.**

Close your class with prayer, asking God to encourage your class members as they seek to live more fully for him.

THE POINT ▶

For Extra Time

HIDDEN IDENTITIES
(up to 10 minutes)

Have adults close their eyes. Give someone a paper clip, a bolt, a pencil, or any obscure object. Allow the person 20 seconds to feel the object and describe it to the rest of the group without naming it or saying what it's used for. Tell the group to make a mental snapshot of the item. Then pass the object around, allowing everyone to silently feel the object, keeping all eyes closed. Repeat the activity with more objects and different describers if time allows. Display the items and have adults open their eyes. Ask:

● **What was it like trying to identify the object from its description?** (I was frustrated; I was confident; I was unsure.)

● **How did your understanding of the objects increase as you were able to experience them more fully?** (The more input we had, the more we were able to understand; seeing is believing.)

Have someone read aloud **John 1:1-18.** Ask:

● **How is what God did by becoming a human like what I did when I let you hold the objects and then look at them?** (People could better understand God; God let people actually experience Jesus.)

Jesus—Human and Divine

Within 500 years after Jesus died, distorted views of Jesus began to arise. As groups emphasized or rejected certain aspects of Jesus' being, differing viewpoints arose. Four of those viewpoints are described on this page. In your group, build a case to defend the view you've been given. Use any Bible passages you can find to support your case, as well as any logical or emotional arguments you can come up with.

Distorted Views

1. *Ebionites* didn't want to believe that a man could also have been God. They
   - denied that Jesus was God;
   - said Jesus was only a man; and
   - believed Jesus gained a special relationship with God when he was baptized and the Holy Spirit came upon him.

2. *Docetists* didn't want to believe that God would have become a human being. They
   - denied that Jesus was human;
   - believed that all matter—the stuff of which all earthly things are made—was evil;
   - claimed Jesus' body was not made of matter, but was some sort of an illusion; and
   - insisted that Jesus, being God, couldn't really have suffered and died.

3. *Arians* believed there was a level of being between humans and God. They
   - denied that Jesus was really God;
   - saw Jesus as inferior to the Father, though superior to human beings; and
   - believed Jesus was the first and highest of all creation, but still a created being.

4. *Nestorians* didn't want to believe that God and a human could exist in the same physical being. They
   - insisted that Jesus' two natures were distinct and separate;
   - said Jesus the human was a different person from Jesus the divine; and
   - claimed that the union between the two persons of Jesus was not biological, but only moral or spiritual.

True View

- Jesus is the Word of God—the complete concept of who God is.
- Jesus is fully God, having existed eternally and having the power and nature of God.
- Jesus is fully human, experiencing all human emotions and temptations.
- Jesus is one being, combining complete humanity and complete divinity.
  See Galatians 4:3-5; Matthew 4:1-11; John 11:28-44; Acts 2:22-33; and Romans 5:6-11.

LESSON 1

God With Us

The Point: ▶ Jesus is God, but he was also fully human.
Scripture Focus: Luke 24:36-49 and John 1:1-18

Reflecting on God's Word

Each day this week, read one of the following Scriptures and examine what that passage says about Jesus' deity or humanity. Then examine how well you are applying the message of that passage in your life. You may want to list your discoveries in the space under each verse.

Day 1: John 2:1-11. Jesus turns water into wine at Cana.

Day 2: Luke 8:22-25. Jesus calms the storm on the Sea of Galilee.

Day 3: Matthew 26:36-44. Jesus prays sorrowfully in Gethsemane.

Day 4: Acts 1:6-11. Jesus ascends to heaven.

Day 5: Colossians 1:15-20. Jesus is head over all things.

Day 6: Philippians 2:5-11. Jesus humbles himself to become human.

Beyond Reflection

1. If Jesus is truly God and truly man, then everything he said should be of extreme interest to all people. Divide the top half of the back of this sheet into two columns. In the first column, list reasons people ignore or reject Jesus. In the second column, list ways you can help others around you overcome those obstacles to begin considering who Jesus really is.

2. Write down five to 10 key views you hold about Jesus, and what response each of those views should cause in your life. Discuss those with someone you trust and ask him or her to hold you accountable for living out the views you've discussed.

3. Since God has done so much for you in sending Jesus as the unique God/man, consider what you might do to spread God's message to others. You might
● set up a prayer time to pray specifically for missionaries who are telling others in your community and around the world about Jesus;
● give time, talent, or resources to help hungry or hurting people—like those Jesus was concerned about in his earthly ministry;
● muster up the courage to gently tell a resistant neighbor how much knowing Jesus has meant in your life.

Next Week's Bible Passages: Matthew 23:1-32 and John 2:12-22

Permission to photocopy this handout from Group's Apply-It-To-Life™ Adult Bible Curriculum granted for local church use.
Copyright © Group Publishing, Inc., Box 481, Loveland, CO 80539.

Lesson 2

A Religious Rebel

◀ **THE POINT**

Jesus challenged wrongdoing and stood up for what was right.

OBJECTIVES

Participants will
- examine what kinds of things make us rebel,
- discover what kinds of things made Jesus rebel,
- experience a rebellion and compare it to Jesus' rebellion, and
- consider what they might do to stand up for what's right.

BIBLE BASIS

Look up the following Scriptures. Then read the background paragraphs to see how the passages relate to adults today.

In **Matthew 23:1-32,** Jesus delivers a scathing denunciation of the religious leaders of the day.

MATTHEW 23:1-32

The same Jesus who had such deep compassion for poor and hurting people couldn't ignore the hypocrisy of the teachers of the law and the Pharisees, who were the Jewish religious establishment of his time. In this passage, he lashes out at them for requiring strict adherence to their long list of rules and regulations, while themselves ignoring the whole spirit of the Scriptures. Jesus pointed out a whole list of examples of the religious leaders' hypocrisy.

- They wanted to make sure they received the honor due them as leaders of the Jewish people (Matthew 23:6-7).
- Not only were the religious leaders neglecting their responsibility to lead people toward God's kingdom, but Jesus says they were even keeping people from entering it

(Matthew 23:13).

• They created petty distinctions governing oaths—saying certain oaths were binding but other similar-sounding oaths weren't. They likely did this so they could make oaths that sounded spiritual and sacrificial—and not be bound by them (Matthew 23:16-22).

• The leaders were proud that they tithed everything, even common household spices, but at the same time they allowed injustice, cruelty, and unfaithfulness to God go unchallenged (Matthew 23:23-24).

• They maintained a righteous and holy appearance, but in truth they were selfish and greedy, taking advantage of others for their own gain (Matthew 23:25-27).

In all of this, Jesus was rebelling against the prevailing religious thought and the establishment of his day. He was saying that we should not be concerned about appearances, wealth, and personal honor—as the religious leaders were. Instead, Jesus was teaching people to be humble servants (Matthew 23:11-12).

Jesus had been patient with the Pharisees and teachers of the Law. He had engaged them in discussion several times, prodding them to see and accept who he really was. But at this late point in his ministry, Jesus chose to confront the sin in their lives. Jesus stood up for what was right even though it meant further rejection by the religious leaders.

JOHN 2:12-22

In **John 2:12-22,** we read the story of Jesus clearing the moneychangers out of the Temple.

Imagine the scene. You're approaching what you consider the holiest place on earth. Suddenly you're hit by the odor of animals and manure. As you enter the outer gates, you see dozens of oxen tied to posts and steaming in the sun's heat. You see pens of sheep everywhere, and cages of doves piled high. The cries of miserable animals fill the air. And at tables all around sit greedy merchants bartering with pilgrims and exchanging foreign money for local currency, making outlandish profits in all their dealings. Jesus rebelled and upset their tables. He drove all the animals from the Temple courts. He rebelled at a system of worship gone wrong.

At the time of the Passover, thousands of Jews came from great distances to worship and offer sacrifices at the Temple. It would have been extremely difficult for these people to have brought animals for sacrifice along on their journey. So it was logical that they be able to buy appropriate animals for sacrifice once they arrived in Jerusalem. However, the sellers were doing two things wrong: They were selling the sacrificial animals within the Temple courts and they were demanding unjust prices from those coming to worship.

Jesus lived by what was right before God, not people. He

knew that the Temple, his Father's house, was to be a place of prayer and worship. Who could have worshiped and prayed in that setting? The people's focus had turned from true worship of God to mechanically fulfilling the requirements of the law. And the religious leaders, who were likely associated with the merchants, were making an unjust profit from the situation as well. Against all that, Jesus rebelled.

There is a time for rebellion—Jesus demonstrated that. But in following his example, we need to be sure that our motives are pure when we choose to rebel—that our choice is based on what we know would be pleasing to God. And we also need to be sure that when the time does come for rebellion we aren't hiding behind bureaucracy or tradition, turning the other way when we see injustice. We need to be able to stand up for what's right as Jesus did, even if it's not the popular thing to do.

THIS LESSON AT A GLANCE

Section	Minutes	What Participants Will Do	Supplies
OPENING	up to 15	**WHAT, ME REBEL?**—Tell a partner something they have rebelled against and estimate how likely they'd be to rebel in certain situations.	
BIBLE EXPLORATION AND APPLICATION	20 to 30	☐ Option 1: **CHARGES OF REBELLION**—Read in Matthew 23:1-32 and John 2:12-22 how Jesus rebelled and formulate "charges" against him.	Bibles, "Righteous Rebellion" handout (p. 38), pencils and paper
	15 to 25	☐ Option 2: **REBELS AMONG US**—Experience how difficult it can be to "go against the flow" and discover from Matthew 23:1-12 and John 2:13-16 how Jesus dealt with the wrongdoing of others.	Bibles, "Behavior Instructions" handout (p. 39)
CLOSING	up to 10	**BEING DIFFERENT**—Read the Beatitudes in Matthew 5:3-12 and examine how we can follow Jesus' example.	Bibles, chalkboard and chalk or newsprint and marker
FOR EXTRA TIME	up to 15	**SERVANT REBELLION**—Read John 13:1-17 and discuss how Jesus wants us to be servants.	Bible

OPENING

What, Me Rebel?

(up to 15 minutes)

THE POINT

As you begin the class, tell adults what they'll be learning in today's lesson. Use the following statement or your own summary of the main point: **Welcome to the second week in our study of Jesus. As you may know, Jesus was not a member of the religious establishment of his day when he lived on earth. In fact, we're going to see today that Jesus was something of a religious rebel.** ▶ **He challenged wrongdoing wherever he saw it and consistently stood up for what was right.**

Since we're talking about rebellion today, let's think about things we've rebelled against. Turn to a partner—not someone who lives with you. Tell that partner about a time you really rebelled at something.

Give adults a couple of minutes, then have several people volunteer to tell what their partners rebelled against. Have them each get the partner's permission first.

Say: **We've all rebelled at some time or another. I have some situations here that I'm going to read to you, and I want to see how likely you would be to rebel in these situations.**

Set up a continuum in the room. Tell adults to go to one end of the room if they would definitely comply in the situation read. Have them go to the opposite end of the room if they would definitely rebel. And have them stand somewhere in between if they are uncertain.

After you read each situation, have people move to the spot they choose on the continuum. Then have them discuss with people near them why they chose to stand where they did and what they would do if they chose to rebel.

Before reading these situations say: **Some of these situations may not exactly fit you. If they don't, try to put yourself in the situation described anyway.**

Situations:

A Christian leader you like and highly respect has asked you and a few hundred other followers to donate $5,000 each toward a new Christian community the leader wants to build.

Your boss comes to you one day and needs you to work four hours over tonight—but you had planned on dinner out with your spouse or someone important to you.

Your fourth-grade son spends about half an hour

32 LESSON 2

a day on homework, and his teacher tells you that he needs to spend more time on it.

Your spouse wants to accept a job in a city 1,000 miles away that you've never seen; you'd have to quit your job, move, and find another job.

Your pastor says every family should bring a grocery sack full of canned goods and a $20 gift certificate for needy families at Christmas.

The president announces a policy promoting "loving termination" of any nonproductive people over 90 years old.

Have adults return to their seats. Say: **Now I'd like you to think about the kinds of things you reacted most strongly to.** Ask:
● **What kinds of things made you rebel most strongly? least strongly?**
● **Who wanted to rebel when I kept making you move to opposite ends of the room? Why or why not?**

Say: **Sometimes it's appropriate to comply with the demands or requests of others. But sometimes we need to rebel. And that's what Jesus did on more than one occasion.**

BIBLE EXPLORATION AND APPLICATION

☐ **OPTION 1:**
Charges of Rebellion
(20 to 30 minutes)

Say: **Probably the most well-known instance of Jesus' rebellion is his clearing of the moneychangers from the Temple. We see another type of rebellion in his confrontation of the religious leaders late in his ministry. Let's take a look at what he did in those situations.**

Form groups of three or four. Have each group choose a reader to read the passage, a leader to keep the group on the task, a recorder to write down the group's responses, and a reporter to share the group's findings with the rest of the class. Assign John 2:12-22 to half of the groups and Matthew 23:1-32 to the other half.

Say: **Your groups are the religious leaders of Jesus' day. In your group, read your assigned passage and come up with at least two charges you could raise**

BIBLE INSIGHT

The "teachers of the law" in the New International Version are called "scribes" in the King James Version and are sometimes referred to as "lawyers." They were scholars whose job was to study and interpret Old Testament law. They tended to "build a fence around the law" by creating rules and regulations designed to keep people from even getting close to breaking the true law. These rules are likely the "heavy loads" Jesus refers to in Matthew 23:4.

Pharisees were members of a particular Jewish religious "party," the most powerful such group of Jesus' day. They tended to be followers of the teachers of the law, themselves being strict proponents of the "letter of the law." Most teachers of the law were also Pharisees, but not all Pharisees were teachers of the law.

LESSON 2

against Jesus. Also, be ready to present why you think you could make the charges stick.

After about five minutes, have groups report their charges and why they think they could make the charges stick.

Then have everyone who studied the John passage stand up and move to stand behind someone who studied the Matthew passage. Have each new pair join another pair to form a new group of four. Distribute the "Righteous Rebellion" handout (p. 38) and have groups discuss the questions on the handout.

After a few minutes of discussion, have groups report.

Then say: **Jesus was definitely a rebel. But what he rebelled against was not the kind of thing we often see people rebelling against today.** ▷ **Jesus challenged wrongdoing and stood up for what was right.**

THE POINT ▷

■■■■■■■■■■■■■■■■■■■■■■■■■

For *Even Deeper* Discussion

Form groups of no more than four and discuss the following questions:

● How is Jesus' rebellion like or unlike the rebellion of the 13 colonies of the United States? to that of Martin Luther? to the crusades of the Middle Ages?

● When is rebellion considered healthy today?

● What can be the costs of suppressing a righteous rebellion?

■■■■■■■■■■■■■■■■■■■■■■■■■

TEACHER
TIP

It's important that you say The Point as it's written or in your own words in each activity. Stating it repeatedly helps adults remember it and apply it to their lives.

☐ **OPTION 2:**
Rebels Among Us
(15 to 25 minutes)

Before class, photocopy and cut apart the slips on the "Behavior Instructions" handout (p. 39).

Say: **I've got a little task for us all to do. Let's get in a circle, and I'll give each of you a slip of paper with your assignment.**

Distribute the instruction slips from the "Behavior Instructions" handout, making sure to have only one of each of the last two. Allow a few seconds for reading the slips, then give adults a signal to begin.

After the happy face is completed and the other "rebellion" has taken place, say: **Your tasks are complete. Thank you.**

Ask the whole class:

● **What did you think of this activity?** (It was kind of silly; I wanted to say something but I couldn't; it was tough to be the only one doing something different.)

34 LESSON 2

● **How did it feel to "go against the flow"?** (Awkward; difficult; I didn't want to do it.)

Form groups of no more than four. Have groups read John 2:13-16 and Matthew 23:1-12 and discuss the following questions. Ask:

● **How were the actions of our "rebels" similar to what Jesus did?** (They did things that were hard; they did what was unexpected; they challenged the status quo.)

● **How were Jesus' actions different from our rebels' actions?** (Jesus was concerned about important things; Jesus really took action and did something good.)

After a few minutes of discussion, have groups report on their discussion.

● **How can we follow Jesus' example?** (By standing up for what we know is right; by not getting stuck on religious rules; by practicing what we preach.)

● **What would it mean in your daily life to "practice what you preach"?** (To be honest in everything; to show the love in work relationships that we see Jesus showing to others.)

● **What might it involve in your workplace or your neighborhood to stand up for what you know is right?** (Confronting someone who steals from the company; telling the boss his actions are unethical; reporting suspected drug activity.)

● **What could be the results of your standing up for what is right?** (I could get fired; people would know I'm honest; I could make people angry.)

Have everyone turn to a partner and tell about one personal experience of someone who really made a difference by standing up for what was right. After partners share for two minutes, have volunteers report instances of people making a difference.

Say: **Jesus challenged wrongdoing and stood up for what was right. We need to follow his example even when it may not be an easy thing to do.**

BIBLE INSIGHT

It appears that Jesus actually drove the merchants from the Temple two different times. The incident we've looked at in John 2 happened very early in Jesus' ministry. But Jesus' actions and message must have fallen on hard hearts. The clearing of the Temple described in the other gospels (Matthew 21:12-13; Mark 11:15-17; and Luke 19:45-46), happened during the week just prior to Jesus' crucifixion.

FOR *Even Deeper* DISCUSSION

Form groups of no more than four and discuss the following questions:

● Can you relate to how the religious leaders felt in today's passages? Explain.

● What good things could we say about these religious leaders?

● How can we avoid the mistakes the religious leaders made in rejecting Jesus?

LESSON 2

APPLY-IT-TO LIFE THIS WEEK The "Apply-It-To-Life This Week" handout helps adults further explore the issues uncovered in today's class.

Give each adult a copy of the handout (p. 40) before they leave and encourage them to take time during the week to explore the questions and activities listed on the handout.

CLOSING

Being Different
(up to 10 minutes)

Have everyone turn to Matthew 5:3-12 and follow along as you read it aloud. Ask:

● **How does what Jesus says in this passage relate to what he said and did in the other passages today?** (Purity of heart is more important than saying all the right things; even though he wants us to be meek, there are times when a situation calls for action.)

● **What can we do to follow Jesus' example of challenging wrongdoing and standing up for what is right?**

As class members call out suggestions, write them on a chalkboard or newsprint. When you have at least 10 ideas on the list, say:

To close our class, lets get back in the pairs we were in earlier. Tell your partner one thing you're going to do this week to work on following Jesus' example of challenging wrongdoing and standing up for what is right. Then pray together that God will help both of you follow through on what you want to do.

 For Extra Time

SERVANT REBELLION
(up to 15 minutes)

Without saying anything, take off your shoes (and socks, if possible). Then read aloud John 13:1-17. Ask:

● **What were you thinking when I took off my shoes and socks and started reading this passage?** (You were going to wash our feet; you were doing an object lesson.)

● **How do you think the disciples felt when Jesus picked up the towel and basin of water?** (Awkward; confused; ashamed.)

● **How did Peter rebel in this passage? Why?** (He didn't want Jesus to wash his feet, because he felt Jesus was too important to wash his feet; he refused to have Jesus wash his feet, because that was a servant's job.)

- **How did Jesus rebel in this passage?** (He did what a servant was supposed to do; he acted as a servant even though he is God.)
- **What kind of wrongdoing did Jesus rebel at in this passage?** (Treating others as less important than us; acting like we should be served by others.)
- **From this example, what kinds of things should we rebel at?** (Being honored above others; thinking too highly of ourselves.)
- **How can we better live out the type of servanthood Jesus demonstrated in this passage?**

Righteous Rebellion

Read the information below describing the religious leaders of Jesus' day. Then discuss the questions that follow.

> The "teachers of the law" in the New International Version are called "scribes" in the King James Version and are sometimes referred to as "lawyers." They were scholars whose job was to study and interpret Old Testament law. They worked to "build a fence around the law" by creating rules and regulations designed to keep people from even getting close to breaking the law. These rules are likely the "heavy loads" Jesus refers to in Matthew 23:4.
>
> Pharisees were members of a particular Jewish religious "party," the most powerful such group of Jesus' day. They tended to be followers of the teachers of the law, themselves being strict proponents of the "letter of the law." Most teachers of the law were also Pharisees, but not all Pharisees were teachers of the law.

1. Putting yourselves in the place of the religious leaders of the day, what would you think of Jesus?

2. What would you think of someone doing something similar in a church today?

3. Thinking of the two passages we've looked at today, what kinds of things really made Jesus rebel?

Permission to photocopy this handout from Group's Apply-It-To-Life™ Adult Bible Curriculum granted for local church use.
Copyright © Group Publishing, Inc., Box 481, Loveland, CO 80539.

■ Behavior Instructions

Make enough copies of this sheet for all class members to have one instruction slip, giving out only one each of the last two instructions.

When I give the signal, sit quietly with your hands folded.

When I give the signal, sit quietly with your hands folded.

When I give the signal, sit quietly with your hands folded.

When I give the signal, sit quietly with your hands folded.

When I give the signal, sit quietly with your hands folded.

When I give the signal, sit quietly with your hands folded.

When I give the signal, sit quietly with your hands folded.

When I give the signal, sit quietly with your hands folded.

When I give the signal, sit quietly with your hands folded.

When I give the signal, sit quietly with your hands folded.

When I give the signal, sit quietly with your hands folded.

When I give the signal, sit quietly with your hands folded.

When I give the signal, sit quietly with your hands folded.

When I give the signal, wait for 10 seconds, then stand up and say, "I'm tired of all this! Why do we even come to this class? I think we should all just go home!" Then sit back down. You'll be the only person doing this.

When I give the signal, go up and erase what's on the chalkboard or turn to a new sheet of newsprint. Then draw a big happy face.

Permission to photocopy this handout from Group's Apply-It-To-Life™ Adult Bible Curriculum granted for local church use.
Copyright © Group Publishing, Inc., Box 481, Loveland, CO 80539.

Lesson 2

A Religious Rebel

The Point: ▶ Jesus challenged wrongdoing and stood up for what was right.

Scripture Focus: Matthew 23:1-32 and John 2:12-22

APPLY•IT•TO LIFE THIS WEEK

Reflecting on God's Word

Each day this week, read one of the following Scriptures and examine what that passage says about rebelling against evil and standing up for what is right.

Day 1: Jeremiah 1:14-19. God tells Jeremiah to take a stand against the evil of his day.

Day 2: 2 Chronicles 20:15-23. Jehoshaphat obeys God against conventional wisdom.

Day 3: Galatians 5:13-26. Paul encourages the Galatians to rebel against their sinful nature.

Day 4: Matthew 5:21-48. Jesus rebels at old sayings.

Day 5: Ephesians 6:10-18. Paul tells us to fight spiritual battles using God's armor.

Day 6: 1 Peter 5:8-11. Peter commands us to resist the devil.

Beyond Reflection

1. Read the entire book of Matthew and list significant teachings Jesus gives us in that Gospel. Then use those teachings to create a profile of the kind of life Jesus would have us live. Grade yourself on how well you're doing at living that life. Talk with a friend about ways you can improve in an area where you gave yourself a low grade.

2. Think about the things you see happening around you at work or in your community. Do you see things that just don't fit with the priorities Jesus has demonstrated to us? Summon up the courage to rebel. Tell God what you think you should do and ask him for the strength to do it. Communicate your commitment to someone you trust and who will encourage you to follow through.

3. For one day, concentrate on being a servant to everyone you encounter. Be extra helpful to your spouse, your children, your co-workers, your employees, your supervisor, your pastor, kids in your neighborhood, motorists on the highway, the clerk at the grocery store, and anyone else you can think of. When people ask why you're acting this way, explain to them that you're trying to be more like Jesus. See how that attitude might change you—as well as those around you.

Next Week's Bible Passages: John 20:1-8; Romans 6:1-14; and Romans 8:31-39

Permission to photocopy this handout from Group's Apply-It-To-Life™ Adult Bible Curriculum granted for local church use. Copyright © Group Publishing, Inc., Box 481, Loveland, CO 80539.

Lesson 3
Our Triumphant Lord

We have hope because Jesus conquered death.

◀ **THE POINT**

OBJECTIVES

Participants will
- discuss why death is sometimes difficult to talk about,
- examine how people changed when Jesus rose from the dead,
- celebrate what Jesus has done for us, and
- consider how Jesus' resurrection should affect us.

BIBLE BASIS

Look up the following Scriptures. Then read the background paragraphs to see how the passages relate to adults today.

In **John 20:1-8,** Mary Magdalene comes to the tomb and finds Jesus' body missing.

JOHN 20:1-8

After her discovery, Mary rushed to tell the disciples what she saw, and Peter and John ran immediately to the tomb. John got there first, but waited outside. When Peter arrived—in his normal, "act now, think later" mode—he walked right in. Apparently he was still trying to figure out what had happened when John came in, saw the evidence, and believed.

Some scholars have drawn interesting conclusions from what this passage says about the position of the grave cloths—for example, concluding that the cloths were lying empty, but in the shape of a body. Some of those conclusions may read too much into the text. However, one thing is clear: From what Peter and John saw, they determined that there had not been a grave robbery; there had been a resurrection!

On Friday, the disciples had been crushed. Jesus had been their hope for a glorious future, but they saw him crucified. They feared for their lives and huddled together in confusion. But Mary's news brought the disciples hope. It's the same hope that drives Christians forward in their faith today. We can cling to the promise of eternal life because Jesus conquered death.

ROMANS 6:1-14

Romans 6:1-14 describes Jesus' victory over death for us.

In the preceding chapters, Paul has explained how the Old Testament law cannot free us from our sins. The law only helps us see that we are sinners. God frees us from sin only by his grace.

Perhaps during Paul's time—and certainly throughout history—some people determined that since we receive more of God's grace when we sin, we should sin all the more so that we can receive more of God's grace! But in this passage Paul explains that our freedom in God's grace doesn't mean that we should sin more so that God can give us more grace. Jesus died for our sins. Our sins went with him to the cross, and he took the punishment for them. And as Jesus rose from the dead, we have new life in him. So we are free to **not** sin. We are no longer bound by the old sinful nature when we are alive in Christ!

As verse 13 says, we "have been brought from death to life." The question is no longer "Why should we refrain from sinning?" but "Why should we ever want to sin again?" God has done such a fantastic thing for us in freeing us from the penalty of death that we should be glad to offer ourselves to be his servants forever.

ROMANS 8:31-39

In **Romans 8:31-39,** Paul explains the wonderful result of what God has done for us through Jesus.

In this passage Paul describes life with Christ in a jubilant song of praise. He explains how we're more than conquerors—how can anything get in our way when God is on our side? We belong to God, who is for us. What an advantage! And we have the promise that nothing can separate us from Jesus' love.

This passage is the ultimate encouragement for us as Christians. Paul's words can both comfort and challenge us as we see the extent of God's love for us.

Through the events that led up to Jesus' death on the cross, we learn much about Jesus' character and his relationship to God the Father. But the most powerful lesson we learn about Jesus comes three days after his crucifixion—when he rises from the dead. As Christians, we can look forward to heaven because Jesus defeated death and because God's love for us will never die.

This Lesson at a Glance

Section	Minutes	What Participants Will Do	Supplies
Opening	up to 10	**Excellent Epitaphs**—Write their epitaphs and discuss the topic of death.	Paper and pencils
Bible Exploration and Application	15 to 25	☐ Option 1: **Full of Joy?**—Examine John 20:1-8 and Acts 2 and determine how the disciples' feelings changed.	Bibles, "What's Going On Here?" handout (p. 49)
	15 to 20	☐ Option 2: **Victory Presentations**—Determine what Romans 6:1-14 and 8:31-39 mean for us today.	Bibles, paper, markers
Closing	up to 10	**Faith Checkup**—Rate their vitality and then thank God for sending Jesus.	Bibles
For Extra Time	up to 10	**God at Work**—Share recent times God has shown his power or love in their lives.	
	up to 10	**Jesus in Our Class**—Discuss questions relating to Jesus and our world.	

THE POINT

TEACHER TIP

If you have more than 15 in your class, you might want to have just six or eight epitaphs read in the whole group for the sake of time.

THE POINT

OPENING

Excellent Epitaphs
(up to 10 minutes)

As you begin the class, tell adults what they'll be learning in today's lesson. Use the following statement or your own summary of the main point: **Welcome to week three in our study of who Jesus is. In today's lesson, we're going to look at Jesus' victory over death. That victory has terrific implications for us as Christians.** ▶ **We have hope because of Jesus' victory over death. Today's lesson will help us understand that victory and will challenge us to live our lives for the One who did so much for us.**

Open with prayer. Then form groups of no more than five. Give each adult a sheet of paper and a pencil or pen. Say: **Here's your chance to leave a message for others to read after you die. Draw a tombstone on your paper and write your epitaph on it. Make it a statement describing how you'd like to be remembered.**

After a few minutes, have adults share their epitaphs within their groups, then have them give their "tombstones" to the person on their left. Gather everyone together and have each person read aloud the epitaph he or she has as if the person were dead.

Ask the whole group:
● **What was it like to read someone else's epitaph in front of the class?** (I felt uncomfortable; awkward; it was pretty strange.)
● **Why is it so difficult to talk about death?** (People are afraid of death; death is an unknown.)
● **Why do people worry about death?** (Because they aren't sure what happens at death; they don't want to leave what they know.)

Say: **Death isn't an easy subject to discuss.** ▶ **But we have hope because Jesus defeated death, and we can celebrate his victory. This lesson will help us learn what Jesus' victory over death means for our lives.**

BIBLE EXPLORATION AND APPLICATION

☐ **OPTION 1:**
Full of Joy?
(15 to 25 minutes)

Say: **Let me set the scene for you. It's a Sunday morning in Jerusalem, about A.D. 30. Jesus was crucified and buried on Friday. We are his**

LESSON 3

disciples, and we're in hiding, fearing that the Jews might come after us now that the Sabbath, Saturday, is over. We're all confused, wondering if we were mistaken about Jesus. Some brave women set out to once more anoint Jesus' body with spices.

Read John 20:1-8.

Say: **When Peter and John return from the tomb, no one knows what to believe. Some are still depressed, but some are hopeful. We're going to see a little bit of what that was like.**

Have people return to their groups. Assign the following roles in each group: Depressed (one who talks only about depressing or sad things), Hopeful (one who tries to bring hope to the conversation), and Followers (all others, who enter the discussion however they see fit). The "What's Going On Here?" handout (p. 49) provides additional Bible information that relates to the disciples' situation. Give each Depressed and each Hopeful person the corresponding section of the handout to help them in their roles.

Say: **Following the instructions for your role, discuss the events that have just taken place.**

If possible, lower the lighting in your room to give the feel of a darkened hiding place. Allow about five minutes for groups to talk. Then get everyone's attention and ask Followers to tell what they observed in the "tone" of their group's discussion.

Ask:

● **Which emotion was stronger in your group: Hope or Depression? Explain.** (Hope, our depressor had a tough time being down; the depressor, he kept thinking of negative experiences.)

● **How are these manufactured feelings like the real feelings Jesus' followers must have had during Jesus' ministry, through his death on the cross, and up to their acceptance of his resurrection? See Mark 16:8 for their feelings upon discovering the empty tomb.** (They must've been unsure how to feel; they didn't know when to be joyful or sad.)

Say: **Following Jesus probably seemed like a roller coaster ride to the disciples. One moment they were incredibly inspired. The next they were confused. And at the same time they were both sad and hopeful. Even after Jesus' resurrection, the disciples experienced incredible feelings of sadness and joy. But joy and hope won out.** ▷ **And we, too, have hope because Jesus conquered death.**

● **In Acts 2, we see the disciples as bold witnesses for Jesus. What made the big difference in the lives of the disciples?** (They'd been confused; they real-

BIBLE INSIGHT

The account in John of the initial discovery of the empty tomb mentions only Mary Magdalene. However, Mary's words in 20:2, "we don't know where they have put him" indicate that there were others with her. Matthew, Mark, and Luke all mention multiple women going to the tomb, with Mark identifying two others: Mary the mother of James, and Salome (Mark 16:1). Those same words of Mary also indicate that at first the women had no thoughts of a resurrection. They were only distressed that they didn't know where the body had been taken.

TEACHER TIP

It's important that you say The Point as it's written or in your own words in each activity. Stating it repeatedly helps adults remember it and apply it to their lives.

◁ THE POINT

ized Jesus had risen from the dead.)
- **How can Jesus' victory over death affect our lives?** (We can build a relationship with God; now we can rise from the dead because he did.)
- **What kinds of things do we regularly do that would be meaningless if Jesus hadn't risen from the dead?** (Pray; worship him; look forward to heaven.)
- **Knowing that Jesus did rise from the dead, what kinds of things should we be doing more often?** (Telling others about him; living to please him; facing death with happiness.)

THE POINT ▷

Say: **Jesus changed his first followers' lives. He turned their unhappiness and frustration into joy and hope.** ▷ **We, too, have hope because of Jesus' victory over death. We can have faith in the one who defeated death for us! And when we have faith in Jesus, he'll make a difference in our lives.**

■■■■■■■■■■■■■■■■■■■■■■■■■

FOR *Even Deeper*
DISCUSSION

Form groups of no more than four and discuss the following questions:
- Some scholars and scientists believe that the Shroud of Turin is actually the cloth Jesus was buried in—and that the image on the cloth was produced by a burst of radiation when Jesus came back to life. If that were proven to be true, how would it affect your faith?
- Is it essential that someone believe in Jesus' bodily resurrection from the dead to be a Christian? Why or why not?
- If someone you know is interested in Christianity but insists that Jesus' resurrection couldn't have happened, how would you try to relate your faith to that person?

■■■■■■■■■■■■■■■■■■■■■■■■■

☐ **OPTION 2:**
Victory Presentations
(15 to 20 minutes)

Form groups of four to six people. Make sure each group has a Bible. Give each group one of the following passages: Romans 6:1-14 or Romans 8:31-39. Then say: **In your group, read the passage and discuss what implications it has for our lives today. Then plan a one-minute presentation based on what you discover. Your presentation can be an explanation of the passage, an examination of its implications, or a celebration of what the passage presents. You can make** your presentation through a skit, an interview, a poster, or any other creative method. In a few minutes, you'll have a chance to lead your presentation in our class.

Provide paper and markers for any groups wishing to make posters. After five to 10 minutes, have groups give their presentations.

Then form pairs and have partners briefly discuss the following questions. Call on members of each group to share their group's insights after you've allowed a few minutes for discussion. Share any insights you feel were meaningful in the Bible Basis section of this lesson.

Ask:

● **Based on what you discovered in the Romans passages, how should our lives be different because of what Jesus has done for us?** (We should live in the Spirit; we should obey God; we should be triumphant over sin.)

● **Why don't our lives always reflect what we read about in these passages?** (Because we let the struggles of life get us down; we let temptations defeat us.)

● **How can we live better for Christ?** (Study the Bible; spend time in prayer; learn from fellow Christians.)

Say: ▶ **We have hope because of Jesus' victory over death. And we can be thankful that our eternal lives are in the hands of the One who has already conquered death.**

◀ THE POINT

FOR *Even Deeper* DISCUSSION

Form groups of no more than four and discuss the following questions:

● What does Paul mean in Romans 8:38 when he says that none of the things he lists "will be able to separate us from the love of God"?

● Can we separate *ourselves* from God's love?

● What effect does Jesus' resurrection have on our future?

TEACHER TIP

The question, "How can we live better for Christ?" could be used for a lengthy discussion. Take as much time as you have available and challenge people to follow through on the good ideas they suggest.

APPLY•IT•TO **LIFE** THIS WEEK

The "Apply-It-To-Life This Week" handout helps adults further explore the issues uncovered in today's class.

Give each adult a copy of the handout (p. 50) before they leave and encourage them to take time during the coming week to explore the questions and activities listed on the handout.

LESSON 3   47

CLOSING

Faith Checkup
(up to 10 minutes)

Form pairs. Have partners share with each other the following sentence completions:

- My faith is strongest in the area of...
- I'd especially like my faith to be stronger in...
- I'll work on improving my faith vitality by...

After a couple of minutes, bring everyone back together. Say: **Knowing what Jesus has done for us should have a major impact on our faith. Let's look at one more passage.**

Have someone read aloud Ephesians 1:15-20. Ask:

- **What does Paul's prayer tell us about the hope we have?**
- **How is God's power at work in our lives?**

THE POINT ▷

Say: ▷ **We have hope because Jesus has defeated death.**

Wrap up your class by having everyone stand in a circle. Have volunteers thank God for what he's done for us through the victorious life, death, and resurrection of Jesus.

For Extra Time

GOD AT WORK
(up to 10 minutes)

Form trios. Have adults share one time recently when they've seen God's power or love at work in their lives. When they're finished, have them pray together, thanking God for his love and for the promise of our resurrection to eternal life with him.

JESUS IN OUR CLASS
(up to 10 minutes)

Form groups of no more than four to discuss the following questions. Then have volunteers share their groups' insights with the whole class.

Ask:

- **If Jesus were physically here with us today, what question would you ask him?**
- **How would people react to Jesus if he began making physical appearances on earth today?**

What's Going On Here?

Make one copy of this sheet for each group of four. Cut apart the two boxes, and give one to each "depressed" person and one to each "hopeful" person.

DEPRESSED

Use the following points to bring the rest of your group around to the same depressed feeling you have.

- The leader you've devoted the last three years of your life to was just executed a couple of days ago on trumped up charges. You saw him die.
- It only makes sense that the people who crucified Jesus would be after the rest of your group next.
- If Jesus' body is gone—and you know you didn't take it—the Jewish leaders or the Romans must be planning some grotesque display of the body to prove Jesus wasn't who he said he was.
- Reports of Jesus' resurrection are pretty hard to believe. People are probably just hallucinating because they'd *like* to see Jesus.

HOPEFUL

Use the following points to bring the rest of your group around to the same hopeful feeling you have.

- Mary and the other women claim angels spoke to them and told them Jesus had arisen.
- Mary says she saw Jesus himself—alive!
- Peter and John say the grave cloths are laying neatly in the tomb. If someone had stolen the body, they wouldn't have messed with removing the cloths first.
- You are beginning to remember some references Jesus made to dying and then rising again.

Permission to photocopy this handout from Group's Apply-It-To-Life™ Adult Bible Curriculum granted for local church use. Copyright © Group Publishing, Inc., Box 481, Loveland, CO 80539.

LESSON 3

Our Triumphant Lord

The Point: ▷ We have hope because Jesus conquered death.

Scripture Focus: John 20:1-8 and Romans 6:1-14; 8:31-39

APPLY·IT·TO LIFE THIS WEEK

Reflecting on God's Word

Each day this week, read one of the following Scriptures and examine how the truths in these passages relate to your life. You may want to list your discoveries in the space next to each verse.

Day 1: Acts 2:22-24. Peter tells about the power of Jesus' resurrection.

Day 2: Acts 3:14-19. Peter encourages repentance.

Day 3: Romans 10:8-11. Paul talks about spreading the good news to others.

Day 4: 1 Corinthians 15:55-58. Paul encourages us to keep serving faithfully.

Day 5: 1 Thessalonians 4:13-18. Paul expresses our hope of Jesus' return.

Day 6: 1 Peter 1:3-9. Peter reminds us of the joy and goal of our faith.

Beyond Reflection

1. Write the words, "Jesus defeated death" on a slip of paper. Put that paper somewhere where you can find it later. Then, when things are really getting you down, take a look at that paper and remember what Jesus' death means for you. It will help you put things in perspective.

2. Plan a small celebration of Jesus' victory over death. Prepare the party for your family or a few friends. Spend much of the time singing praise songs or talking about what God has done for you. Enjoy the great news that Jesus defeated death as you discuss what heaven might be like.

3. Determine one thing you'll do this week to help someone else along on their road to faith in Christ. It may be telling someone what Jesus has done for you, it may be explaining how to make a faith commitment to Christ, or it may just be helping someone who's hurting get through a struggle—as you reflect Christ's love.

Next Week's Bible Passages: James 1:22-25 and selected passages from Acts

Permission to photocopy this handout from Group's Apply-It-To-Life™ Adult Bible Curriculum granted for local church use.
Copyright © Group Publishing, Inc., Box 481, Loveland, CO 80539.

Lesson 4

Teacher for All Time

Jesus' teachings can have a powerful impact on our lives.

◀ **THE POINT**

OBJECTIVES

Participants will
- discuss effective teaching methods,
- examine how Jesus changed people 2,000 years ago,
- explore how Jesus has affected history, and
- consider how seriously they apply Jesus' teachings.

BIBLE BASIS

Look up the following Scriptures. Then read the background paragraphs to see how the passages relate to adults today.

In **James 1:22-25,** James addresses two major issues related to the teachings of the Bible.

JAMES 1:22-25

The two issues James concentrates on here are the importance of studying the Bible and the perhaps even greater importance of putting what we've learned from Scripture into practice. James says that we are blessed through the careful, consistent study of the teachings of Scripture and the application of those teachings to our lives.

James is emphatic in encouraging us to be doers of the Word and not just hearers. The Greek word *akroatai,* which is translated "hearers," indicates a person who listens to a lot of lectures—perhaps those of many different teachers—but has never become a committed follower of anyone. A term we might use in a similar way would be "seekers." James might say that people who don't incorporate the Bible's teachings into their lives are simply seekers—ones who've never really become disciples. James would likely say these people are deceiving themselves if they think they're doing what God wants them to do.

In churches today, many people sit through a class and a sermon on Sunday morning, and then go home and concentrate on other things in their lives—failing to put any spiritual learning that has taken place into practice. Perhaps these people are deceiving themselves, as James points out. According to this passage, we will receive great blessing in our lives when we not only study the Bible regularly, but obey God's teachings as well.

SELECTED PASSAGES FROM ACTS

In the selected passages from Acts, we see examples of how Jesus' life and teachings affected his followers after his resurrection.

In **Acts 4:1-13,** Peter and John are put in jail for teaching about Jesus. When brought before the high priest, Peter boldly confronted the Jewish leaders with the truth about Jesus and his resurrection. The leaders' response was interesting: they were amazed at the courage of Peter and John, and "took note that these men had been with Jesus."

Acts 4:32-35 tells of how early believers shared everything they had. In this example, Jesus' teachings had so changed these people that they were selling anything they had to help the poor among them. They took Jesus' teachings seriously. It was this nucleus of people who took Jesus' message to those around them and began to make a real difference in the world.

In **Acts 5:17-32** and **40-42,** we read how the apostles rejoiced at the opportunity to suffer for Christ. This group of people realized what Jesus had done for them. Having been put in jail because of the jealousy of the high priest and his cronies, the apostles were miraculously released by an angel in the night. Instead of going into hiding, they were in the temple courts again the next day, preaching the message of Jesus.

It's interesting that though the Pharisees and Sadducees (the two main religious parties of the day) seldom agreed on anything, when the apostles were brought before the Sanhedrin (the Jewish ruling council), they agreed to flog the apostles and order them not to preach about Jesus! After being confronted by the Sanhedrin, the apostles went away praising God. They were so changed by Jesus that they were proud to suffer persecution for him.

Acts 17:16-34 tells the story of Paul before the meeting of the Areopagus in Athens. The Areopagus was a ruling council for the city of Athens during Paul's time, though the council's authority was strictly limited by the Roman government. In this meeting of extremely important people who believed in all kinds of pagan gods, Paul—formerly a

Christian-hater—explained how the true God was the God who created the world, the God of the Bible. When he mentioned the resurrection of the dead, he raised quite a stir. Though the Greeks believed in the immortality of the soul, the idea of dead bodies coming back to life seemed absurd to them. Paul boldly, though carefully, prepared the way to present Jesus to them—and several of them believed!

In this study we're concentrating specifically on the impact of Jesus' teachings, which are the heart of God's message to us. Jesus was an incredible teacher. He knew how to get people thinking about the important issues of life. As we examine the impact Jesus' teachings can have on our lives, we'll be motivated to spend more time discovering and seeking to obey what Jesus has given us.

This Lesson at a Glance

Section	Minutes	What Participants Will Do	Supplies
Opening	up to 15	**Our Most Effective Teachers**—Tell about teachers who were particularly helpful and list characteristics of effective teachers.	
Bible Exploration and Application	15 to 25	☐ Option 1: **Looking in the Mirror**—Look in a mirror and compare their experience to what is described in James 1:22-25.	Small mirror, Bibles, paper and pencils, chalkboard and chalk or newsprint and marker, 3×5 cards
	20 to 30	☐ Option 2: **Changed!**—Conduct "TV interviews" with people referred to in selected passages in Acts and examine how Jesus has affected history.	Bibles, "Jesus in History" handout (p. 60)
Closing	up to 10	**Taking Action**—Ask God to help them follow Jesus' teachings better in a particular area.	Bibles
For Extra Time	up to 10	**Course Reflection**—Describe what they've learned from this course.	
	up to 10	**A Closer Look**—View the room through a small hole and discuss how our discoveries relate to studying Scripture.	3×5 cards, nail
	up to 15	**Parable Power**—Examine Jesus' parable of the seeds.	Bibles, chalkboard and chalk

OPENING

Our Most Effective Teachers
(up to 15 minutes)

As you begin class, tell adults what they'll be learning in today's lesson. Use the following statement or your own summary of the main point: **Welcome to the fourth and final week in our series on who Jesus is. In this study, we're going to concentrate on Jesus as the teacher for all time and learn how ▷ Jesus' teachings can make a difference in our lives.**

THE POINT ▷

Open with prayer. Then encourage class members to get involved in the discussions and activities during the study.

Form groups of no more than six. Have each adult tell the group about one teacher that was particularly helpful to him or her and why. They may want to talk about school teachers, relatives who were excellent teachers of everyday knowledge, or work associates who trained them in some way.

When all groups are finished, bring everyone back together and compile a list of characteristics of good teachers.

Then ask:

● **How did Jesus demonstrate these characteristics?**

Say: **Jesus is a master teacher. He used extremely effective teaching methods while he was here on earth. But more important to us than his methods is his message. ▷ Jesus' teachings can have a powerful impact on our lives. They can lead us to the life God wants for his people.**

THE POINT ▷

TEACHER TIP

It's important that you say The Point as it's written or in your own words in each activity. Stating it repeatedly helps adults remember it and apply it to their lives.

BIBLE EXPLORATION AND APPLICATION

☐ OPTION 1: Looking in the Mirror
(15 to 25 minutes)

Pass a small mirror around your class, allowing everyone to look into it for a second or two. When it has gone all the way around, ask:

● **What do you remember about what you just saw in the mirror?** (How bad I look this morning; how big my nose is; how much I need a haircut.)

● **If you saw something in the mirror you didn't like, what could you do to change it?** (Get a haircut; spend more time on my makeup; comb my hair.)

Form groups of four or five and give each group paper

54 LESSON 4

and a pencil. Have each group choose a reader to read James 1:22-25, a recorder to jot down notes on their discussion, a reporter to share with the rest of the class, and one or two encouragers to keep the discussion going. Allow groups about five minutes to discuss these questions.

Ask:

● **How are we deceiving ourselves when we "merely listen to the word"?** (We think we're doing OK because we're learning God's Word; we think about how right a passage is, but then we forget to act on it.)

● **How does James' simile of looking at a mirror and then forgetting what you look like connect with his message?** (Sometimes we think we look a lot better than we really do; we don't always do what it takes to make ourselves look better.)

● **How does this passage relate to learning from Jesus' teachings?** (We need to study the Bible to learn; we need to act on what we learn.)

● **How can studying Jesus' teachings result in our being blessed?** (If we do what he wants us to, he will lead us into what is best for us; he guides us through his Word.)

Have groups report their responses to these questions, then ask:

● **What specific things can we do to help ourselves better apply the things we learn about?**

Have your class list all the things they can think of in two or three minutes. Write their responses on a chalkboard or newsprint.

After two or three minutes, pass out 3×5 cards and have adults each write on a card one thing to work on in the coming week.

Say: ▶ **Jesus' teachings can have a real impact on our lives. As we study them carefully, they help us understand what Jesus wants for us and give us encouragement to follow him wholeheartedly. Keep your note card in front of you somehow this week and concentrate on doing what you've chosen to do.**

BIBLE INSIGHT

Scholars interpret James' mirror simile in several different ways. Many feel he's talking about just a fleeting glance into a mirror, not really stopping to see the details. Another more likely interpretation is that the person looking into the mirror doesn't bother to look deeper than the skin. He only sees what's on the surface and doesn't seem to be concerned with the deeper issues of who he really is or how his beliefs should affect his actions.

TEACHER TIP

If adults have trouble thinking of ways to help them do better, get them started with these suggestions: Writing on a note card what action we want to take and keeping it with us through a day or a week; really studying the Bible more instead of just reading it; asking someone to hold us accountable.

◀ THE POINT

■ ■

For *Even Deeper* Discussion

Form groups of no more than four and discuss the following questions:

● How does James' emphasis on action relate to Paul's emphasis on faith? (See Ephesians 2:8-10.)

● What kinds of blessings do you think James refers to in James 1:25?

● Read James 1:27. Where does the study of Jesus'

teachings fit into James' description of pure and faultless religion?

■■■■■■■■■■■■■■■■■■■■■■■■■■■

☐ **OPTION 2:**
Changed!
(20 to 30 minutes)

Say: **Remember from last week how frightened and confused Jesus' followers were before his resurrection? Today we're going to look at what happened after the resurrection.**

Form pairs. Assign one of the following passages to each pair: Acts 4:1-13; Acts 4:32-35; Acts 5:17-32 and 41-42; and Acts 17:16-34.

Say: **In a moment we're going to conduct some live TV interviews. Decide which of you in your pair will be the interviewer and which will be the interviewee. The interviewer will be reporting for WWHY TV in Rome around A.D. 40-50. The interviewee will be someone who was present in the situation described in your passage.**

Have partners read their passage together and choose two or three interview questions that will bring out the effect that Jesus and his teachings have had upon the person or people in their passage. As partners are preparing, you might want to go to each pair and share information from the Bible Basis that is significant to the pair's passage.

Give partners about five minutes to read and prepare, then have them present their interviews.

After the presentations, ask:

● **What was it like to put yourself into the shoes of a first century Christian?** (Awkward; strange; fun; frightening.)

● **For those of you who were here last week, did these people seem like some of the same people we read about then? Explain.** (No, they acted totally different; yes, last week they were just beginning to understand what had happened.)

● **What changed these people?** (They discovered that Jesus really had risen from the dead; they realized Jesus was for real after all.)

● **How was the effect of Jesus and his teachings on those people's lives like the effect he has had on your life?** (He's changed me totally; living by his teachings gives me meaning in life.)

● **How was it different?** (They were changed more dramatically because they actually lived with Jesus and saw him after the resurrection; I don't get as excited as they did.)

Say: **We've talked about Jesus' life and his teachings**

TEACHER TIP

If you can provide a real microphone for the interviewer (even if it's not connected), it will add realism to the interview. Or use a carrot or other similar-shaped object for a bit of realism and even more fun!

having an effect on his followers. The reason we've combined those two things is that we can't really separate Jesus' life from his teachings—he consistently lived what he taught. And Jesus' life and teachings have had a tremendous effect throughout history. Let's look at some things people have said about Jesus since about the year 1500.

Distribute the "Jesus in History" handouts (p. 60). Say:

Read through this sheet silently. Choose your favorite quote of a sentence or two. Be prepared to tell what quote is your favorite and why.

Give adults about two minutes to read the quotes. Then go around your class and have people report their favorite quotes and why they like them. If you have more than nine in your group, divide into groups of five to eight for sharing favorite quotes.

Have people remain in their groups to discuss these questions. Ask:

● **What effect has this study had on your perception of the influence of Jesus' teachings?** (It's reminded me of the influence he's had; it makes me realize how he should have more influence in my life.)

● **How can we take Jesus' teachings more seriously in our lives?** (Spend more time studying them; practice what we say we believe; remember all he's done for us.)

● **Why should we take Jesus' teachings more seriously in our lives?** (Because he's given them to us for our good; because of all he's done for us; because he loves us and wants to help us.)

Say: **Jesus changed our world. Take a look at the handout again. Look at the dates of people's lives and quotes. Every year listed is in relation to when Jesus was born. All of history points either forward or backward to Jesus. No other person has made an impact even remotely close to that! However, many people in history have spoken highly of Jesus and his teachings—and even followed them—without ever having the personal relationship with God that is available to us through Jesus. Jesus' teachings can have a tremendous impact in our lives if we commit ourselves to him and diligently follow the guidelines for living he has given us.**

For *Even Deeper* Discussion

Form groups of no more than four and discuss the following questions:

● Respond to this statement and explain your response: Jesus' influence in the world is rapidly decreasing in our age and culture.

● Could any decline we see in Jesus' influence be related to how well his followers are living out his teachings? Explain.

● What can we do to increase Jesus' influence in our culture? What *should* we do?

■■■■■■■■■■■■■■■■■■■■■■■■■■■

APPLY·IT·TO LIFE THIS WEEK

The "Apply-It-To-Life This Week" handout helps adults further explore the issues uncovered in today's class.

Give adults copies of the handout (p. 61) before they leave and encourage them to take time during the coming week to explore the questions and activities listed on the handout.

CLOSING

Taking Action
(up to 10 minutes)

Say: **Take a moment right now to privately consider how seriously you take Jesus' teachings. Think about the things we've just discussed and ask yourself how you can better allow Jesus' teachings to have more of an impact in your life.**

Form pairs. Have partners share one area they would like God's help in following Jesus' teachings better. Then have them briefly pray together, sharing their requests with God.

THE POINT ▷

When all have prayed, say: ▷ **Jesus' teachings can have a tremendous impact in our lives. But the words are meaningless unless we follow them with our actions. Let's read Psalm 143:8-10 together as a closing prayer.**

Read from the translation most popular with your class. Be sure everyone can see a Bible of that translation and read the passage aloud together. At the end, give your own "Amen."

Ask adults what they liked most about the course and what they'd like to see different about it. Please note their comments (along with your own) and send them to the Adult Curriculum Editor, Group Publishing, Inc., Box 481, Loveland, CO 80539. We want your feedback so we can make each course we publish better than the last. Thanks!

For Extra Time

COURSE REFLECTION
(up to 10 minutes)

Have adults reflect on the past four lessons. Have them take turns completing the following sentences:
- Something I learned in this course was...
- If I could tell friends about this course, I'd say...
- Something I'll do differently because of this course is...

A CLOSER LOOK
(up to 10 minutes)

Tell people to take a look around the room to see what their surroundings are like. Then give each person a 3×5 card in which you've poked a hole with a medium-sized nail. Then say: **Take the next couple of minutes to observe the detail in things in this room by looking only through the hole in your card. Choose something you discover and make a mental "snapshot" of the item.**

After a couple of minutes, have adults form groups of no more than four and tell what "picture" they took. Have adults discuss the following questions in their groups:
- **What new things did you notice as you looked through the hole in your card?**
- **How are your discoveries like the discoveries Jesus' disciples may have had while learning from him?**
- **What can we learn from this activity about how to study Jesus' teachings?**

PARABLE POWER
(up to 15 minutes)

Say: **Jesus often used parables in his teaching. Let's look at one particular parable that also relates to the influence of Jesus' teachings.**

Form groups of no more than four. Have them read Mark 4:3-8 and 13-20 in their groups. As they read, write the following incomplete sentences on a chalkboard or newsprint:
- Jesus taught this parable because...
- A parable was a good way to teach this idea because...
- A new insight I gained from our study of this parable is...

Say: **In your groups, discuss this passage using these sentence starters as the core of your discussion. Be sure everyone in the group contributes to your discussion.**

Give groups about five minutes for their discussion. Then bring everyone back together and ask:
- **What insights did you gain from this study of the passage?**
- **How does this parable relate to the depth of the impact Jesus has in people's lives?**

Jesus in History

By a Carpenter mankind was made, and only by that Carpenter can mankind be remade.
—Desiderius Erasmus (1466-1536)

He who shall introduce into public affairs the principles of primitive Christianity will change the face of the world.
—Benjamin Franklin (1706-1790)

I know men; and I tell you that Jesus Christ is no mere man. Between him and every other person in the world there is no possible term of comparison. Alexander, Caesar, Charlemagne, and I have founded empires. But on what did we rest the creations of our genius? Upon force. Jesus Christ founded his empire upon love; and at this hour millions of men would die for him.
—Napoleon Bonaparte (1769-1821)

Civil society was renovated in every part by the teachings of Christianity. In the strength of that renewal the human race was lifted up to better things. Nay, it was brought back from death to life.
—Pope Leo XIII, May 15, 1891

As the centuries pass the evidence is accumulating that, measured by his effect on history, Jesus is the most influential life ever lived on this planet.
—Kenneth Scott Latourette, American Historical Review, LIV, January, 1949

The simplicity and charm and yet the depth, the directness, the universality, and the truth of his teaching made a deep mark on his hearers, and elicited the conviction that they were in the presence of a Teacher such as man had never known before. The same impression has been made in every age since the days of Christ and his immediate followers, and in any full consideration of his person as the substance of Christianity great attention must necessarily be paid to his teaching.
—Griffith Thomas, *Christianity Is Christ*, 1965

Jesus Christ is the outstanding personality of all time.... No other teacher—Jewish, Christian, Buddhist, Mohammedan—is *still* a teacher whose teaching is such a guidepost for the world we live in. Other teachers may have something basic for an Oriental, an Arab, or an Occidental; but every act and word of Jesus has value for all of us. He became the Light of the World. Why shouldn't I, a Jew, be proud of that?
—Sholem Ash in Christian Herald.

For 2,000 years, he *has* been the Light of the World, and his words have *not* passed away.
—Henry M. Morris, *The Bible Has the Answer*, 1971

LESSON 4

Teacher for All Time

The Point: ▶ Jesus' teachings can have an impact on our lives.

Scripture Focus: James 1:22-25 and selected passages from Acts

APPLY▪IT▪TO LIFE THIS WEEK

Reflecting on God's Word

Each day this week, read one of the following Scriptures from Jesus' Sermon on the Mount and examine how Jesus' teaching in that passage can be applied to your life. You may want to list your discoveries in the space next to each verse.

Day 1: Matthew 5:1-12. Jesus gives guidelines for Christlike behavior.

Day 2: Matthew 5:13-16. Jesus says we are to be salt and light to our world.

Day 3: Matthew 5:27-32. Jesus warns about sexual sin and divorce.

Day 4: Matthew 5:33-48. Jesus teaches about promises, revenge, and love.

Day 5: Matthew 6:5-15. Jesus gives a pattern for prayer.

Day 6: Matthew 6:19-34. Jesus reminds us to keep our priorities straight.

Beyond Reflection

1. For Jesus' teachings to have any affect on our lives, we first have to study them. Choose a specific time to spend studying God's Word. It can be any time of the day or night, and it doesn't have to be a long time. Start with 10 minutes, if that's all you can afford. If you're already doing more, that's great. Increase the time you spend in God's Word as you see it having a positive effect in your life. If you study the same passages as a friend or family member, meet periodically to talk about your insights.

2. If you're studying God's Word regularly, use a method mentioned in the lesson to help you apply it to your life: Write one principle you've picked up each time you study and put it on a 3×5 card. Put that card where you'll see it during the day, such as on the refrigerator or the dashboard of your car. Keep all the cards and review them from time to time to see how you're doing.

3. Read Matthew and list significant teachings Jesus gives us in that Gospel. Then re-read those teachings and create a profile of the kind of life Jesus would have us live. Grade yourself in the areas listed on your profile. Talk with a trusted friend about ways you can improve your grade in an area where you scored yourself with a low grade.

Permission to photocopy this handout from Group's Apply-It-To-Life™ Adult Bible Curriculum granted for local church use. Copyright © Group Publishing, Inc., Box 481, Loveland, CO 80539.

Fellowship and Outreach Specials

Use the following activities any time you want. You can use them as part of (or in place of) your regular class activities, or you can plan a special event based on one or more of the ideas.

What Do You Do Besides Work?

Have all class members bring an object that represents something they like to do other than work. Someone might bring a softball to represent playing sports, a spark plug to represent tinkering with cars, or a spool of thread to represent sewing. The items can be as big or small as anyone wants to bring. Let each adult explain his or her item and tell one fun experience related to the item or the topic it represents.

You might take this activity a step further by discussing how we could use our hobbies to draw others to Jesus.

Jesus Is . . .

Have adults create a multimedia program on Jesus for the whole church. Include such elements as interviews with Christians about their relationship with Christ, segments of videos that depict Christ, music about Jesus, and stories or skits about Jesus. Be sure to obtain the proper permissions for any copyrighted materials you use.

Advertise and present the program to the whole church. Or arrange to present it in a more public place as an outreach tool.

Passion Play

Create your own passion play (a drama about Jesus' life, death, and resurrection) as a special adult project. Enlist the help of people with dramatic expertise and let your class pull it all together. Take advantage of people's gifts and talents—not everyone is an actor or actress. Some will be more suited to building sets, sewing costumes, designing programs, or doing publicity.

Make your production as intimate or as colossal as you want. You could even make it a dinner-theater presentation and raise money for a worthy cause. Be sure to have class members invite non-Christian friends and co-workers.

Giving It Away

Do something bizarre: give something away. Have your class get together and make things to be given away to adult friends and co-workers. You might make baked goods, Christmas ornaments, craft items, or other creative gifts. Have individuals choose who to give the gifts to and be sure everyone encloses a personal note, explaining that you're giving these gifts simply to reflect Jesus' love.

Christmas Any Time

Hold a Christmas party, even if it's July! Center everything around Jesus and what he means to us. Play and sing Christmas carols, eat Christmas treats, and bring gifts. Only don't exchange the gifts; take them to an organization that will distribute them to homeless or needy people. Take time to let people tell about their most meaningful Christmas, about a time they really experienced the joy of being a Christian, or about how much Christ means to them. Close by singing "Joy to the World."